D0462856

Warren G. Harding

Kent, Deborah.
Warren G. Harding :
America's 29th president
2004.
WITHDRAWN
3305208153902
h   01/21/05

G. Harding

Deborah Kent

AMERICA'S
29TH
PRESIDENT

Children's Press®
A Division of Scholastic Inc.
New York / Toronto / London / Auckland / Sydney
Mexico City / New Delhi / Hong Kong
Danbury, Connecticut

SANTA CLARA COUNTY LIBRARY

3 3305 20815 3902

Library of Congress Cataloging-in-Publication Data

Kent, Deborah.
      Warren G. Harding / by Deborah Kent.
          v. cm.—(Encyclopedia of presidents)
Includes bibliographical references and index.
Contents: The boy from Marion—The rising star—A man of the party—
The senator from Ohio—Back to normalcy—The legend and the truth.
  ISBN 0-516-22965-6
    1. Harding, Warren G. (Warren Gamaliel), 1865–1923—Juvenile literature.
2. Presidents—United States—Biography—Juvenile literature. [1. Harding,
Warren G. (Warren Gamaliel), 1865–1923. 2. Presidents.] I. Title. II. Series.
E786.K46 2004
973.91'4'092—dc22   2003027883

© 2004 by Deborah Kent
All rights reserved. Published in 2004 by Children's Press,
an imprint of Scholastic Library Publishing.
Published simultaneously in Canada.
Printed in the United States of America.

CHILDREN'S PRESS and associated logos are trademarks and or registered
trademarks of Scholastic Library Publishing. SCHOLASTIC and associated
logos are trademarks and or registered trademarks of Scholastic Inc.
1 2 3 4 5 6 7 8 9 10 R 13 12 11 10 09 08 07 06 05 04

Contents

One   7
The Boy From Marion

Two   17
The Rising Star

Three   29
A Man of the Party

Four   43
The Senator From Ohio

Five   59
Back to Normalcy

Six   79
The Legend and the Truth

Presidential Fast Facts   96
First Lady Fast Facts   97
Timeline   98
Glossary   100
Further Reading   101
Places to Visit   102
Online Sites of Interest   103
Table of Presidents   104
Index   108

Chapter 1

Winnie

On a July day in 1882, 16-year-old Warren Harding mounted his father's mule. He had recently graduated from a small local college and had stopped to visit friends in Caledonia, Ohio. Now he set out on the mule to join his family, which had just moved to the Ohio town of Marion, 9 miles (14 kilometers) away. He remembered that muleback journey for the rest of his life.

"I started out early in the afternoon," he recalled, "but this mule had only one gait." The old mule was going slower than Harding could have traveled at a leisurely walk. As the sun began to sink in the west, Warren stopped at a farmhouse and asked an old man how far it was to Marion. The old man answered, "Well, if you are going to ride that mule, it is a farther distance than you will ever get."

Harding stuck with the mule, and as the last rays of light disappeared from the western sky, he heard the evening church bells of

Marion. "I do not know that I have ever heard a concert of bells that sounded so sweet," he concluded.

Harding was pleased to be moving to Marion. He had been a farm boy all his life, and he was eager to experience life in town. Three major railroads crossed in Marion, bringing passengers and freight from all points of the compass. The town offered more things to do and new people to meet. Warren Harding hoped to build his future in Marion.

Just as he hoped, Warren Harding prospered in Marion. He became one of the town's leading businessmen, and his success led him into politics. Even when he reached the highest office in the nation, he felt strongly tied to Marion. He remained a man from small-town Ohio, a man who followed the American dream to the heights.

Early Life

Warren Gamaliel Harding was born on November 2, 1865, in a farmhouse near Corsica, Ohio (now called Blooming Grove). Corsica was about 25 miles (40 km) east of Marion, and his early life would play out along the road between the two places. Harding was named Warren Gamaliel after one of his father's uncles. His mother had wanted to name him Winfield, and she called him by her own affectionate nickname, Winnie.

Phoebe and George Tryon Harding, Warren Harding's parents.

The firstborn of eight children, Warren was his mother's joy. "Winnie is always walking," she wrote to her sister when her son was a year old. "He will walk all along the walls. . . . It is an impossibility to get his picture taken. We have tried several times, but to no effect—he won't sit still." When he was four, she taught him his letters. She was convinced that he had special gifts and was destined to do great things. Phoebe Harding liked to boast that her son Warren would someday be president of the United States.

At school and on the streets of Corsica, Warren was sometimes taunted by the other children. Pointing out his dark complexion, they called him a Negro. The rumors that the Hardings had African American ancestors followed them wherever they went. Warren's father, George Tryon Harding (known as Tryon), claimed that an enemy of the family started these rumors out of spite. Tryon Harding fiercely denied that his family had any African American ancestors.

Tryon Harding was a reluctant farmer. He was eager to leave the cornfields and milk cows behind him forever. For a few years he taught school, but lessons and noisy children were not to his liking either. When Warren was young, his father studied at the Homeopathic Hospital College and set up a medical practice in the nearby town of Caledonia. His medical practice never flourished. His few patients paid in eggs and butter more often than hard cash. Phoebe Harding brought in some extra income by serving as a *midwife*, helping neighbor women during childbirth.

When he wasn't setting broken bones or stitching wounds, Tryon Harding poured his energy into trading. He bought and sold farm implements, livestock,

Harding (center) at about seven years old.

and even businesses, always trying to earn a profit. When Warren was ten, one of his father's trades brought him a failing local newspaper, the Caledonia *Argus*. Warren began helping out in the newspaper office. He swept the floor, cleaned the printing press, and learned to set and sort type. One night, after Warren had put in especially long hours, the paper's editor gave him a present. It was a 2 1/2-inch (6-centimeter) printer's rule, a symbol of the printer's craft. Warren treasured this gift and kept it all his life.

College Days

By the time he was 14, Warren had gone as far as he could in the local schools. His parents scraped up the money to send him to a local college. Warren enrolled at Ohio Central College, about 7 miles (11 km) from Caledonia, in the village of Iberia. Warren's father had graduated from the same school about 20 years earlier. Ohio Central College was more like a small high school than a modern college. There were only three teachers, and about 35 boys and girls between the ages of 13 and 16.

Course selection at Iberia was limited. The students studied philosophy, Latin, mathematics, and science. Warren took little interest in his classes, but he threw himself into school activities. One of his roommates recalled that Warren's main interests were debating, writing, and making friends. In school debates

Warren discovered a talent for public speaking. He adored high-flying phrases, and his expressive voice captivated his audience no matter what the topic.

Warren's early experience with the Caledonia *Argus* gave him a love of newspapers. With the help of a friend, he founded a local paper for students and townspeople called the Iberia *Spectator*. The first issue appeared in February 1882. Its four pages were crowded with local news, jokes, advertisements, and commentaries on national issues. The *Spectator*, which came out every two weeks, was a big success. In an editorial Harding wrote gleefully, "The *Spectator* is taken by every family in our city excepting a few stingy old grumblers who take no more interest in home enterprise than a mule takes in a hive of bees."

Warren enjoyed his years at the school immensely. In later life, he wrote, "I am still persuaded that the smaller college, with the personal contact between the members of the faculty and student body, was the best educational institution of which we have ever been able to boast."

Warren was one of three students who graduated from Iberia in the spring of 1882. He delivered the commencement address and received the degree of bachelor of science. While he was finishing his last term, his family moved from Caledonia to Marion. After a stop in Caledonia, Warren set out on the mule for Marion, ready to begin a new life.

In Search of a Calling

When Warren Harding arrived in 1882, Marion, Ohio, was a thriving town of some 4,500 people. It was the seat of Marion County, home of the courthouse and the county jail. One of the town's biggest employers was a company that manufactured hay rakes, reapers, and other farm implements. Beyond the city limits spread cornfields, orchards, and patches of woodland and marsh.

A few weeks after his arrival, Warren Harding began his first full-time job, as schoolmaster in the White Schoolhouse, a one-room school much like the one he had attended in Caledonia. "It was the hardest job I ever had," Harding recalled. He resigned even before the school year was over. In February 1883, he wrote to his aunt, "Next Friday one week [a week from Friday], forever my career as a pedagogue will close, and—oh, the joy! I believe my calling to be in some other sphere and will follow out the belief."

Tryon Harding suggested that perhaps Warren should study law. He arranged for his son to study under the guidance of a Marion attorney. "I entered the office with misgivings," Harding wrote to a friend years later. "Lashing my feet to the top of a desk and tilting back in a chair, I glued my eyes on *Blackstone* [a major law text] four or five hours a day. It was slow work and money ran out." The law was not Harding's sphere, either.

What Harding really loved was loafing about with his numerous friends. Still in his teens, he played cornet in a local band that provided music for Marion's popular roller-skating rink, the Merry-Roll-Round. He stayed out until late at night, joking and telling stories. One of his favorite pastimes was the game of poker. For the rest of his life Harding's "poker buddies" were among his closest friends. Harding also began to take an interest in Republican politics. He

Harding always loved music and claimed he could play nearly any band instrument. Here he tries out the sousaphone during his years in the White House.

attended party rallies and helped with campaign jobs. He found that making friends was an important part of political life—a part that was easy for him.

Harding tried his hand at selling insurance. Almost at once he made a major sale. The company soon realized, however, that Harding had miscalculated the rates and undercharged the customer. He was forced to pay the difference out of his own pocket. The insurance venture, too, ended in failure.

In May 1884, Dr. Harding's trading skills landed another floundering newspaper, the Marion *Daily Star*. The town had two other newspapers, but one appeared only weekly and the other was published twice a week. The *Star*'s main assets were a hand-operated printing press and enough lead type to set the pages of a single edition. With an 18-year-old's enthusiasm, Warren Harding jumped at the chance to become the *Star*'s editor. It would be his job to find enough news every weekday, to sell advertising to businesses willing to pay, and to find local people to subscribe.

Chapter 2

Beating the Odds

As editor of the *Star*, Warren Harding received free passes from railroad companies that passed through Marion. The railroads were hoping for favorable coverage from the *Star*, and Harding used the passes to help cover the news. A month after he took over the paper, he rode a train to Chicago to attend the 1884 Republican National Convention. There he was thrilled by the crowds, the speeches, the bands, the banners and balloons. He was most taken by James G. Blaine, the former senator from Maine who won the Republican nomination for president. When Harding returned to Marion, he was a fierce Blaine supporter. Soon afterward he delivered the first campaign speech of his career.

Harding was hoping to promote candidate Blaine in the *Star*, but just at that moment Tryon Harding was forced to sell the paper in

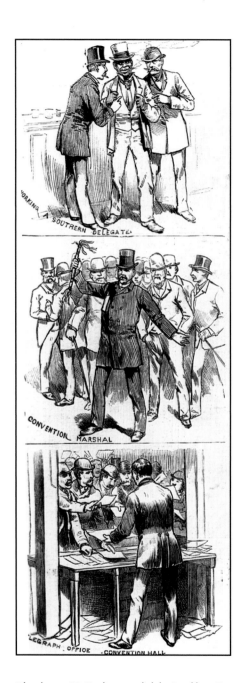

When he was 18, Harding attended the Republican National Convention in Chicago. The excitement of the convention may have helped steer him toward politics.

order to pay a debt. The *Star* closed, and Warren Harding was out of a job. He went back to playing cornet in the skating rink band and trying again to sell insurance. His father persuaded the editor of another Marion paper, the weekly *Mirror*, to give Warren a job, but within a few weeks Harding was fired. The *Mirror* editor said that Warren spent too little time reporting the news and too much time helping the Blaine campaign for president.

That fall, when James G. Blaine lost the presidential election, Harding and his friends were sitting in a Marion saloon wondering what to do next. Together, they came up with a great idea. Harding, Jack Warwick, and Johnnie Sickle realized that if they pooled their money, they could buy the Marion *Star*, and Harding could continue his newspaper career. Harding had to borrow part of his share from his recent employer, the editor of the *Mirror*. Before the end of November, the first edition of the new *Star* rolled off the press.

Harding was the big winner in the deal. Johnnie Sickle soon lost interest in the newspaper and eventually sold his share to Harding. Harding won Jack Warwick's share in a poker game but persuaded Warwick to stay on as a reporter. At the age of 19, Harding became the *Star*'s owner and editor.

The old *Star* published mostly human-interest stories, comic strips, and light verse, mostly material reprinted from other newspapers. Harding had more ambitious ideas. He began running articles on the front page about national

The Marion *Star* building, where Harding published his newspaper, becoming a familiar and popular figure in the town.

politics and international relations. He also began running stories on local people and events. He understood that his readers loved recognition. He made it his policy that the name of each Marion citizen should appear somewhere in the *Star*'s pages at least once a year.

The new improved *Star* gained notice and praise. In February 1885, the Delaware (Ohio) *Chronicle* wrote, "The little twinkling *Star* at Marion has at last fallen into good hands. Marionites could do no better thing than [to give] it a most liberal support." In May the *Star* moved to a larger office. Soon Harding launched a second paper, the *Weekly Star*. In the daily paper, the editor did not express strong political views, but the *Weekly Star* had definite Republican leanings. In it, Harding could express his own judgments and opinions.

The Marion Booster

In the 1880s and 1890s, the United States was stretching its arms and flexing its muscles. Villages were growing into towns, and towns were blossoming into cities. Railroads crisscrossed the countryside. New factories were creating new products and new opportunities for owners and workers alike.

Warren Harding understood this, and he was eager to see Marion get its fair share. Wherever he went, he tried to sell Marion and its advantages. At home, he urged his readers to take pride in their town and contribute to its growth. "Talk about Marion—write about Marion—be friendly to everybody," he urged in 1887. "Sell all you can—buy all you can at home—support your town newspaper—advertise!"

Harding insisted that Marion outshone every other town in central Ohio. In 1888, only half in jest, he wrote, "There is wicked Kenton—we're always ahead of her; sleepy Marysville is not to be compared; Mount Gilead, compared to Marion, is as copper to gold; Mount Vernon is a fair country town, but we knock her silly."

Harding put in 12- and 14-hour days to run the paper. He gathered stories, sold advertising, and supervised the typesetting and printing. Yet the busy office still had an easygoing atmosphere. Harding still had time to sit with his big feet (he wore size 14 shoes) on his desk, chewing tobacco and swapping stories with friends who dropped by. Sometimes he hired a wandering hobo as a printer for a few weeks. The wanderer was allowed to sleep on a cot in the back room. One day a big shaggy dog wandered in and he stayed for years. Harding named him Senator.

In 1890 Harding threw himself into a campaign for civic improvement. City streets in those days were crude dirt roads. During the spring thaw or after a big rain, they became huge sinks of mud. Harding urged Marion to pave its streets. "Get Marion out of the mud!" became his slogan. Paving could be funded by taxing the property owners who lived along each street. Not surprisingly, many property owners objected. Harding was outraged. He accused the opposition of standing in the way of progress. In a blazing editorial, he wrote, "They are not now, never have been, and never will be of any earthly use to Marion. . . . Let the drones get out! . . . Marion wants to move onward."

Romance and Marriage ——————————

One of Harding's fiercest opponents on the paving issue was Amos Kling, a powerful Marion businessman. Kling was one of the richest men in town, and he hated Warren Harding. He was outraged when Harding began to court his daughter Florence.

Tall and handsome, with a winning smile and jovial manner, Warren Harding was immensely popular with the young women of Marion. He could have selected almost any girl in town to be his wife. On the surface, Florence Kling seemed an odd choice. She was a homely, ungraceful woman five years his senior. She had a shrill, commanding voice and a sharp tongue. Furthermore, she had been married before. She had divorced her husband, Henry De Wolfe, after he abandoned her and their infant son. In the 1890s, most people looked down on divorced women. Harding, however, was not troubled by Florence's unhappy past. She adored him, and she yearned to help him rise in the world. Her ambitions for him matched (some would say, even surpassed) his ambitions for himself.

Amos Kling was determined to stop his daughter from marrying Warren Harding. In an effort to destroy Harding's reputation, he stirred up the old

Florence Kling Harding was an able and intelligent woman. Warren Harding relied on her judgment and advice.

Florence Mabel Kling was born in Marion in 1860. She studied music in Cincinnati, then returned to Marion, where she taught piano. Harding probably first met her when she was giving lessons to his sister Charity. After they were married, Florence became the business manager of the Marion *Star*. She organized a crew of boys to deliver papers, and was known to spank them if they became unruly. Because of her regal manner Harding nicknamed his wife "the Duchess." The nickname stuck for the rest of her life.

★★☆

rumor that the Harding family had African blood. Florence was as strong willed as her father. She wanted to marry Harding, and nothing her father said could stop her.

Florence Kling and Warren Harding were married on July 8, 1891. Amos Kling refused to attend the wedding. Kling shunned his daughter and son-in-law for the next seven years.

Shortly after the wedding, Harding began to suffer severe bouts of stomach pain, especially at night. Within a few months he had what he later called a "nervous breakdown." For treatment he went to the Battle Creek Sanitarium, a famous treatment center in Michigan. A few weeks later, he returned to Marion

The Harding home in Marion, which remained the couple's permanent address throughout their lives.

rested and restored. Over the next ten years he had four more such incidents, each time seeking treatment at Battle Creek.

The town of Marion was growing into a small city, and the *Star* became its most successful paper. Warren and Florence Harding built a comfortable green-shingled house on Marion's Mount Vernon Avenue, which would be their home for the rest of their lives. The boy who had ridden into town on a balky mule had become one of Marion's leading citizens.

The Bedrock Conservative ───────────

Like many self-made men, Harding took a *conservative* view of government. He had worked hard at the *Star*. He had been rewarded with a substantial income and a measure of prestige in the community. Harding looked up to other self-made businessmen. He believed that society benefited when businesses were allowed a free rein. Furthermore, he was convinced that men who gained great wealth were particularly suited for political power. "It is undoubtedly true," he wrote in December 1889, "that nine out of ten statesmen who possess great fortunes have earned their money themselves by the exercise of those qualities of energy, industry, and enterprise which have likewise made them prominent in politics."

While ambitious and energetic businessmen were making fortunes, however, millions of workers and poor farmers were struggling to meet their basic needs. During the 1880s, industrial workers began to organize trade unions to pressure employers to provide better wages and safer working conditions. When negotiations broke down, the workers sometimes went out on strike. Harding had no patience for labor unions or those who organized them. In his editorials,

Harding called union organizers "demagogues" and contended that they posed a threat to society. He was also opposed to strikes and applauded non-union workers.

Harding was also not friendly to reformers who were seeking to improve the world through new laws. Some fought for the right of women to vote. Others wanted to restrict the sale of alcoholic beverages or end the death penalty for criminals. Harding took a conservative position on all these issues. For example, he opposed laws against the sale of alcohol, insisting that it was up to the individual, not the government, to control alcohol use.

Still, the *Star* was cautious about controversial issues. "We did not let the paper dabble in reform," Jack Warwick wrote years later. "It tried simply to be decent, respectable, and reliable, minding what little business it had to mind." As the years passed, Harding spent less time in the office of the *Star*. His interest in Republican politics led him to seek office himself.

Chapter 3

On the Campaign Trail ——————————

"I am a candidate for the Republican nomination for state senator in the 13th District," Warren Harding announced in the *Star* on July 5, 1899. "As a candidate I would like to be considered on merit—on availability [and] capacity as a Republican who has cared to be only a private in the ranks and has stayed there through thick and thin."

Harding won the party nomination and began campaigning for the senate seat. At rallies in towns all over the district, he dazzled his listeners with his speeches. People loved to hear his voice, no matter what the topic. As one admirer explained, his talk "always made the occasion pleasanter."

One night during his campaign, Harding stayed at a rundown hotel in the village of Richwood. At the pump in the yard he met a fellow guest, Harry M. Daugherty. Daugherty, like Harding, was

Harry Daugherty became the first supporter of Harding's political ambition and remained a close adviser the rest of Harding's life.

active in Ohio's Republican party. He had served two terms in the state legislature. Though he no longer held office, Daugherty worked quietly behind the scenes, supporting Republican candidates and promoting bills. Years later he recalled his first meeting with Warren Harding. He watched Harding's handsome figure cross the yard of the inn and thought, "What a great-looking president he'd make!"

The Democrats were strong in Harding's home county, but the other counties in the district usually voted Republican. In those counties he received wide support. On the night of the election, the Hardings opened their house to friends and well-wishers. When the news came in that Harding had won, a brass band struck up a rousing rendition of a popular song, "There'll Be a Hot Time in the Old Town Tonight." So many people crowded onto the Hardings' front porch that it collapsed beneath their weight.

In winning his first political race, Harding had been helped by his ability to stay on good terms with the Republican factions trying to gain control of the party in Ohio. One was headed by U.S. Senator Joe Foraker, who had also served two terms as governor of Ohio. His rafter-shaking speeches earned him the nickname "Fire Alarm Joe." The other faction was led by U.S. Senator Mark Hanna, a wealthy businessman from Cleveland who had helped Ohioan William McKinley win the U.S. presidency in 1896. Harding, never one to encourage disputes within the party, kept peace with both sides and gained their support for his election.

On January 1, 1900, Harding moved into a suite of rooms in Columbus, the Ohio capital, which was only 40 miles (64 km) from Marion. He took his place in the Ohio State Senate, which met in a vast, high-ceilinged room with massive desks, deep leather armchairs, and crystal chandeliers. It was a striking

The two feuding leaders of the Ohio Republican party: Senator Joseph "Fire Alarm Joe" Foraker (left) and Marcus Hanna (right), a wealthy industrialist from Cleveland.

contrast to the office of the *Star*, with its clattering presses and resident dog.

Harding adapted to his new life with ease. He set out to make friends with other

senators and with a large group of Republicans in the city. One of them was Harry

M. Daugherty.

To the men of the Ohio legislature (there were no female members in 1900) Harding was a good companion, "one of the boys." He was always ready with a joke and always eager for a game of poker. He welcomed any excuse to drop in at the nearest saloon. When political opponents quarreled, he invited them out for an evening of fun. In a legislature torn by feuds, Harding was a master at patching up differences. In the fall of 1901, he ran for a second term and was easily re-elected.

State senator Warren Harding.

In 1903 the Republicans nominated Cleveland banker Myron Herrick to run for governor. They chose Warren Harding to run on the ticket for lieutenant governor. The ticket had the united support of the party and ran on the slogan, "Herrick, Harding, and Harmony." Herrick and Harding won election. Soon afterward, party unity disappeared, and Republican factions began bickering again. Harding, as lieutenant governor, did his best to serve as a peacemaker, but had little success. When Herrick and Harding ran for re-election in 1905, they lost to a strong Democratic challenger. Herrick returned to his business in Cleveland, and Harding returned to the *Star* in Marion.

Public Life, Secret Passion ———————————

Back in Marion, Harding spent time in his office, gossiping with old friends who stopped by. During the next few years, he seized every opportunity to travel. He took a long trip to Florida one winter, and in the summer visited New England and Nova Scotia. During the summers, he sometimes went from town to town, giving paid lectures on the "Chautauqua circuit." One of his favorite topics was "The Life of Alexander Hamilton." Harding deeply admired Hamilton, who was the American founding father most interested in economics and business. Hamilton believed that the United States could become a great industrial nation, and he urged the national government to help and protect private business. Now, a hundred years later, Harding felt that Hamilton's vision of America was becoming a reality.

In 1905, while Warren Harding was still lieutenant governor, Florence Harding became gravely ill. Doctors decided that one of her kidneys must be removed. In the age before antibiotics, it was highly risky surgery. Florence spent five months in a Columbus hospital, much of the time in excruciating pain.

The Chautauqua Circuit

In an era before movies, radio, and television, "Chautauqua lectures" were a popular form of summer entertainment. A tent was set up, and tickets were sold for lectures by distinguished people on a wide variety of subjects. Chautauqua visitors might learn about Greek mythology, African art, the kings and queens of France, or almost anything else. Chautauqua evenings also featured interludes of entertainment. These acts might include singers, acrobats, or even trained animals.

☆ ★ ☆

During the worst of her illness, Harding was at her bedside. As she began to recover, however, he went back to Marion.

In the evenings he began visiting Carrie Phillips, the wife of a Marion businessman. Carrie's husband, Jim Phillips, was one of Harding's friends, but he was away recovering from an illness himself. Carrie was intelligent and attractive. She was everything Florence was not—young, graceful, and vivacious. Over the next 15 years, Harding and Carrie Phillips conducted a secret love affair. When they were apart, he wrote her poems and heartfelt letters, some of them 50 and 60 pages long.

Florence Harding knew that her husband was tempted by the charms of other women, yet for years she remained unaware of his relationship with Carrie

A Chautauqua gathering. Political leaders, educators, and entertainers spoke to hundreds at these educational events. Many in the audience were women.

Phillips. In 1909 the Hardings and the Phillipses even took a ten-week tour of Europe together. Florence continued to play an essential role in Harding's life, and the public was never aware of any problem between them. Florence shared her husband's ambitions and was always there to urge him on. In every new endeavor she stood by his side.

New Challenges

During the early 1900s, the national Republican party became increasingly divided. In 1901 Theodore Roosevelt was sworn in as president after the death of William McKinley. Roosevelt was the leader of the *progressive* wing of the Republican party, and as president, he gained wide public support. He increased government regulation of business and exercised more government control over the nation's land and resources. In 1908, Ohioan William Howard Taft was elected president, promising to continue Roosevelt's policies.

By 1909, conservative Republicans were working to regain control of the party. Yet even in Ohio, the growing progressive wing of the party was reluctant to compromise with the "old guard." In these difficult circumstances, the party nominated Warren Harding as a compromise candidate for governor. Harding was a conservative at heart, but he rarely expressed strong views on controversial subjects, so he remained acceptable to progressives.

The people of Marion were elated by the rise of their native son. On the night before the election, 3,000 Harding supporters streamed through the streets of Marion in a "pre-victory" parade. Standing before his house on Mount Vernon Avenue, Harding waved to delegations from dozens of neighboring towns. Flags flew, and nine marching bands blared out patriotic music. Placards read: BOOST A BOOSTER! VOTE FOR HARDING, MARION COUNTY'S SON!

Harding was sure that he would win. When the votes were tallied, however, he was defeated by Democratic governor Judson Harmon. Harding had gravely underestimated Harmon's appeal, and he was stunned by his loss. He felt betrayed by the people of Ohio and told friends he would leave politics forever. Yet within a few weeks he took a more philosophical approach. He wrote to a friend, "I have lost nothing which I ever had except a few dollars which I can make again, a few pounds of flesh which I can grow again, a few false friends of whom I am well rid, and an ambition which simply fettered my freedom and did not make for happiness."

Toward a Wider Arena

In the summer of 1912 Harding went to Chicago as a *delegate* to the Republican National Convention, representing his Ohio district. President Taft had the support of most conservatives and hoped to win the nomination for re-election.

Former president Theodore Roosevelt was running for the nomination, supported by the party's progressive wing. Harding strongly supported Taft, and he was chosen to place Taft's name in nomination. Roosevelt supporters hissed and booed when Harding rose to speak. As he praised Taft's virtues, fistfights broke out in the hall. Despite the turmoil, Harding finished his speech to thunderous applause. Taft won the Republican nomination, but Roosevelt ran as the candidate of the new Progressive party. They split Republicans' votes, and Democrat Woodrow Wilson was elected president.

Harding's involvement in national politics kept his personal ambitions alive. In 1914 he won his party's nomination for the U.S. Senate, defeating his old mentor Joe Foraker. The Democratic candidate was Ohio's attorney general, Timothy S. Hogan. In largely Protestant Ohio, Hogan was an Irish Catholic. Anti-Catholic feeling was a strong force in the United States in 1914, and Harding's supporters used it to full advantage. An anti-Catholic rhyme appeared on walls and posters:

Read the Menace and get the dope.

Go to the polls and beat the Pope.

Harding never mentioned Hogan's religion, but he did not stop his supporters from raising the issue at every opportunity. Harding defeated Hogan by

At the 1912 Republican National Convention, Warren Harding delivered the nominating speech for William Howard Taft. Taft won the nomination but lost the election to Democrat Woodrow Wilson.

100,000 votes. His Senate term did not begin until December 1915, more than a year away. He used the time to indulge his love of travel. He and Florence visited friends in Texas, crossed the Southwest to California, and sailed to Hawaii. In Hawaii they met a handsome, charming naval engineer named Charles R. Forbes, who was supervising the construction of the military base at Pearl Harbor. Both Warren and Florence Harding found Forbes a delightful companion, and they resolved to keep this new friendship alive.

In November 1915, the Hardings moved into a big brick house on Wyoming Avenue in Washington. Soon Harding would begin a new phase of his life as a member of the U.S. Senate, but walking the streets of the nation's capital he was swept with homesickness. "I think I am going to like the work done here," he wrote to a friend, "but I confess a longing every afternoon to get a whiff of the hurly and bustle of the newspaper shop at home."

Chapter 4

A Man for All Seasons —————————

Warren Harding had come a long way from Marion, Ohio. The editor

of the Marion *Star* sat in the Senate Chamber, where for more than a

century statesmen had shaped the nation's history. Harding was

thrilled and honored to be among the rich and powerful members of

the Senate, but his small-town background ill prepared him to deal

with matters of national and international importance.

Making up for his lack of knowledge about the issues, Harding

fell back on his personal charm. He quickly made friends with the

other senators. "By nature he was a conservative," wrote New York

senator James Wadsworth Jr. years later, "but he kept his mind open

toward genuinely progressive movements." What Wadsworth saw as

an open mind, however, was Harding's reluctance to take a stand when

controversy arose. When a debate on a controversial subject was

Florence and Warren Harding in Washington after his election to the U.S. Senate.

announced, Harding often did not show up for it. Yet if a reform measure was certain to pass, Harding raised his hand in its favor. When it was clear that most Republicans favored giving women the right to vote, Harding voted for *women's suffrage*. He personally opposed the *prohibition* of alcoholic beverages, but in Congress he voted for Prohibition to appease his anti-saloon *constituents* (the people of Ohio, whom he represented in the Senate).

During his six years in the Senate Harding introduced 134 bills, none of which was very important. Nearly all of them were local bills, benefiting residents in Ohio. Among his national proposals were bills for the celebration of the landing of the Pilgrims, distribution of tents to the homeless, support for teaching of Spanish in the public schools, and the preservation of the Ohio birthplace of President William McKinley. Harding's few political actions had one important virtue—they made him no enemies.

Party leaders remembered Harding's stirring nomination speech for Taft in 1912, and in 1916 they chose him to be chairman of the national convention in Chicago. They also asked him to give the keynote address, setting the themes for the convention. The party's progressive wing had lost much of its power, and the Republicans were more unified than they had been in years. Still, the delegates seemed bored and listless. Their party was out of power (Democrat Woodrow

Bloviating

Warren Harding sometimes used the word *bloviate* to describe his skill at public speaking. He saw it as the art of speaking eloquently without saying anything controversial or upsetting to the audience. Many journalists of the time criticized him severely for the empty quality of his speeches. Senator William McAdoo once described a Harding speech as "an army of pompous phrases moving across the landscape in search of an idea."

☆ ☆ ☆

Wilson was president), and they seemed to have no promising candidate to run against him.

Harding tried to rouse the convention with his soaring oratory, but the delegates only yawned and fidgeted. By the end of his two-hour speech, the hall was nearly empty. A reporter for the *New York Times* wrote that "a convention of oysters" could have listened with greater enthusiasm. Harding was deeply discouraged. His strength as a public speaker had failed him. To a friend he confessed, "Since the roasting I received at Chicago, I no longer harbor any too great self-confidence in the matter of speech-making."

War had raged in Europe since the summer of 1914, but the United States had remained neutral. By early 1917, pressure for the country to go to war against Germany was growing rapidly. Harding would have to vote on any declaration of war. Then he received a letter from Carrie Phillips, his secret love in Marion. Carrie, who had recently spent two years in Berlin, had deep German sympathies. She warned Harding that if he spoke in favor of war against Germany, she would make public the huge collection of love letters he had sent her. She would shatter his marriage and his political career.

In April, President Wilson asked Congress for a declaration of war. Support for the declaration was almost unanimous. One after another, members of Congress rose and gave patriotic speeches. When Harding spoke, however, he was unusually subdued. "It is my deliberate judgment that it is none of our business what type of government any nation on this earth may choose to have," he stated. "The German people evidently are pretty well satisfied with their government." He went on to celebrate America's fight for justice and right. Perhaps Carrie Phillips was satisfied with his speech. Even though he voted in favor of the declaration, she continued to keep his love letters a secret.

Old Friends and New

In May 1917, Harding received a letter from a young woman named Nan Britton. Britton, who grew up in Marion, wrote from New York, "I wonder if you will remember me." Six years earlier, when she was 14 years old, Nan Britton had developed a crush on Harding. She trailed him around town, finding endless ways to attract his attention. Now, she told him, she had moved to New York and had been working as a typist. She asked if Harding could help find her a job.

Harding replied. He told her he was coming to New York the next week and would like to meet with her. "You see, I do remember you," he concluded.

Soon after the meeting, Harding got Nan Britton a job in a Washington office, and they began to meet regularly, sometimes in Harding's senate offices. When they were apart, he wrote her long passionate letters, much like the ones he wrote to Carrie Phillips. In 1919 Nan gave birth to a daughter, Elizabeth Ann. She told Harding that he was the child's father. Harding never saw Elizabeth Ann, but he regularly sent Nan Britton money for the child's support. According to many accounts, Harding continued to see Nan Britton after he became president. Their long

Nan Britton wrote a book after Harding's death, claiming that he was the father of her daughter, born when Harding was a U.S. senator.

affair was not publicly known during Harding's lifetime. It came to light in a sensational book that Nan Britton published in 1927.

Harding maintained other ties with old friends in Marion. He brought George Christian, the son of a Marion neighbor, to serve as his private secretary in Washington. Christian became a devoted assistant and friend. He kept track of Harding's appointments, answered letters, and provided a touch of home in the busy capital.

In the meantime, Warren and Florence Harding became well-known figures in Washington society. Harding hosted frequent poker parties at his home on Wyoming Avenue, enjoying hours of good talk while Florence served snacks and drinks. In return for their hospitality, the Hardings received numerous invitations to parties at the homes of Washington politicians.

Ohio congressman Nick Longworth and his wife Alice Roosevelt Longworth were among the most dazzling couples in Washington. Alice was the daughter of former president Theodore Roosevelt. She was famous for her irreverent sense of humor. At a White House party she once whispered to a fellow guest, "If you can't say anything nice about anybody, come sit by me." At one of the Longworths' high-society parties, the Hardings met Ned and Evalyn McLean. The McLeans had inherited fabulous fortunes, and their extravagance knew no

Alice and Nick Longworth became friends with the Hardings in Washington. Alice Longworth was the daughter of former president Theodore Roosevelt. Nicholas Longworth was a congressman from Ohio.

bounds. They owned newspapers, railroads, and other businesses and lived in high style. Evalyn loved expensive jewelry, and the famous Hope diamond was among her treasures. Despite their wide differences, Florence Harding and Evalyn McLean formed an enduring friendship.

The Compromise Candidate ————————

In 1918, the armies of the Allied Powers began driving German armies out of Belgium and France. On November 11, 1918, the German government asked for an *armistice*, an end to the fighting. Millions of soldiers and civilians had been killed, and the world's people were eager to avoid another such terrible war.

President Woodrow Wilson of the United States proposed an ambitious plan to avoid future wars by establishing a world organization called the League of Nations. In December 1918, Wilson sailed to France to take part in the peace negotiations and gain support for his plan. During the negotiations, he was forced to make many compromises, but the final treaty, signed in June 1919, called for the establishment of the League of Nations.

Wilson returned to the United States only to learn that many Americans were wary of the new organization. They argued that the United States should take care of its own concerns and stay clear of the problems of other countries. They feared that membership in the League of Nations could actually draw the United States into another war. Opposition to the League of Nations was led by Republican senator Henry Cabot Lodge, the powerful chairman of the Senate Foreign Relations Committee.

Wilson set out on an ambitious speaking tour to urge U.S. membership in the league, but Senator Lodge followed behind, arguing against it. Harding sided with Lodge and other leading Republicans. In a Senate speech, he said, "It is my deliberate conviction that the League of Nations Covenant . . . either creates a super-government of the nations which enter it or it will prove the colossal disappointment of the ages. I cannot believe this republic ought to sanction it in either case." Spectators cheered his declaration.

Exhausted, President Wilson gave up his speaking tour and returned to Washington. Soon afterward, on October 2, he suffered a serious *stroke* (blockage of blood flow in the brain) which paralyzed his left side. He spent the remaining 17 months of his term secluded in the White House, physically and emotionally broken.

During Wilson's last years as president, American voters grew weary of debates over the League of Nations. They blamed Wilson and the Democrats for involvement in the European war and for the downturn in the economy once the fighting ended. It was becoming clear that the Republicans had a strong chance to elect a Republican president in 1920. The big question was who they would nominate.

Former president Theodore Roosevelt was hoping to run, but he died suddenly in 1919. His death left the field wide open, and a host of candidates surged forward. General Leonard Wood, a longtime friend of Roosevelt, was seen by many as his natural successor. Another strong contender was Illinois governor

In 1919, President Woodrow Wilson traveled the country urging United States membership in the League of Nations. Harding and many other Republicans opposed him.

Frank Lowden. Conservative Republicans thought that Wood and Lowden were too progressive, however. Republican leaders wanted a candidate who would bring back solid conservative government and would work with party leaders to encourage business and reduce government spending. Some suggested that Senator Warren Harding might be just the man they were looking for.

At first, Harding backed away whenever anyone suggested his candidacy. He preferred to stay in the Senate, he insisted. The presidency would be an overwhelming burden to him. Harding's old friend Harry Daugherty was determined to make him change his mind. One evening, while Harding was in Ohio during a congressional recess, Daugherty invited him for a visit. The two men talked for six hours or more. Finally Harding asked the key question, "Am I a big enough man for the race?"

"Don't make me laugh!" Daugherty exclaimed. "The [day] of giants in the presidential chair has passed."

As Daugherty hoped, Harding agreed to enter the race. Though Wood and Lowden seemed to have more popular support, Daugherty was convinced that Harding could win the nomination as a compromise candidate who could satisfy dissenting groups within the party.

"I don't expect Senator Harding to be nominated on the first, second, or third ballot," Daugherty told a reporter, "but I think about eleven minutes after two o'clock on Friday morning of the convention, when fifteen or twenty men, bleary-eyed and perspiring profusely from the heat, are sitting around a table some one of them will say: 'Who will we nominate?' At that decisive time the friends of Senator Harding can suggest him and can afford to abide by the result."

A reporter later pictured the scene as a room hazy with cigar smoke, and the legend was born that Harding was nominated by a group of party insiders in a "smoke-filled room." Daugherty's prediction came true almost exactly. After Wood and Lowden deadlocked in the early balloting, a group of Republican senators gathered in a suite at Chicago's Blackstone Hotel to discuss the situation. Of all the possible candidates, Warren Harding seemed the least problematic. At a few minutes past two in the morning, they agreed to support him.

The next morning, one of the senators took Harding aside and asked him whether there was anything in his history that might embarrass the party. Harding said he needed some time to think. Perhaps he pondered his love affairs with Carrie Phillips and Nan Britton or the occasional chest pains that had begun to plague him. Yet after ten minutes of consideration, he told the senator that there was nothing in his past that would endanger his run for the presidency.

Harding supporters rushed from one state delegation to the next, bargaining and persuading. Dozens of delegates who had pledged to stand by Lowden, Wood, and other candidates agreed to make Harding their second choice. On the

Harry Daugherty and Warren Harding during the 1920 presidential campaign.

tenth ballot, the Kansas and Pennsylvania delegations shifted their votes to Harding, giving him the majority needed for the nomination. The band played, the crowd cheered. Postcards with Harding's portrait, tossed from the balcony, fluttered to the floor like snowflakes.

Harding joined in the excitement. He laughed and joked with well-wishers who pressed around him, fighting to shake his hand. Thinking of poker, his favorite game, he remarked, "We drew to a pair of deuces and filled." (He meant that he didn't have a very good hand to start with, but was lucky to draw good cards and win his bet.)

As Harding's running mate, the convention chose Massachusetts governor Calvin Coolidge, who had gained national recognition in 1919 by acting with firmness to end a strike of policemen in Boston. Coolidge and Harding could hardly have been more different, but they shared two important qualifications. Both men had basically conservative Republican views, and neither had made any powerful enemies.

Oddly, the Democrats nominated another Ohio newspaper publisher, James M. Cox, to run against Harding. Cox, who owned papers in Dayton and Springfield, was a progressive Democrat who supported U.S. membership in the League of Nations and had served three terms as governor of Ohio. The voters appeared to be tired of progressive reforms and international involvement, however. Unless unforeseen disaster occurred, Harding's victory seemed assured.

Chapter 5

The Front Porch Campaign

In Marion, Ohio, it was as though the circus had come to town on a Fourth of July that lasted all summer long. The Marion Civic Association set up a "Victory Way" from the Union Depot to Harding's home on Mount Vernon Avenue. The visitors who streamed to the candidate's house passed between eagle-topped columns and saw photos of Harding smiling from every window. Bands played, flags flew, and streamers billowed from rooftops.

Harding sat on his front porch (rebuilt since its collapse ten years before) and greeted the visitors who arrived by the thousands. He smiled and joked with reporters. He signed autographs, chatted with old friends, and charmed nearly everyone with his easy good nature. Florence Harding kissed babies and patted little girls on the head. Harding modeled his "front porch campaign" on those of two

Warren Harding addresses a crowd from the front porch of his home in Marion during the summer of 1920. He addressed thousands of visitors during his "front porch" campaign.

earlier Ohio candidates for president, James Garfield and William McKinley. Harding supporters moved a flagpole from McKinley's front lawn in Canton and planted it in front of Harding's house.

Harding's campaign strategy was to give the impression that he was "just folks," an honest, ordinary man whom Americans could trust. President Roosevelt had been a famous author and world traveler. Woodrow Wilson had been a college professor and scholar. By contrast, Harding was a small-town businessman with familiar small-town views. In a campaign speech, he promised "not heroics, but healing; not nostrums, but normalcy; not revolution, but restoration; not agitation, but adjustment; not surgery, but serenity." The most important word was "normalcy," promising a return to a simpler and less demanding time.

Harding's campaign was managed by Will H. Hays, chairman of the Republican National Committee. Hays set up headquarters in New York City, with a network of offices around the country. Harding supporters fanned out across the country supplied with a wealth of materials to deliver the party message and polish Harding's image. Harry Daugherty, Harding's longtime supporter, ran the campaign office in Marion.

In late summer Harding left his porch and set off by rail on a "whistle-stop tour." Crowds cheered him in Minneapolis and Des Moines, St. Louis and Chattanooga. The *Daily Oklahoman* reported that Harding's visit to Oklahoma

"America First," the slogan on this Harding poster, expresses Republican opposition to membership in the League of Nations.

City was "the noisiest, gladdest, maddest day" the Republican party had ever seen in that usually Democratic state. Harding spoke in school auditoriums, American Legion halls, and town squares. Sometimes he addressed his eager listeners from the rear platform of his special railway car, the *Superb*.

The Harding campaign portrayed Democrat James Cox as a candidate with ties to corrupt Democratic bosses in Ohio. It also worked to connect him with President Wilson and the war. One political cartoon showed Cox, as Wilson's chauffeur, driving into the mud, while Harding gallantly pointed toward the main road.

Though the odds were strongly in Harding's favor, his support team was on guard against trouble. Soon after Harding's nomination, Will Hays arranged to send Carrie Phillips and her husband on a round-the-world cruise. Carrie had tried to blackmail Harding once, and the committee wanted her safely out of the way during the presidential campaign. Harding continued to send generous payments to Nan Britton for the support of little Elizabeth Ann. Nan remained discreetly silent.

Harding also had to face the charge once again that some of his ancestors were African Americans. In 1920, the charge was dangerous to Harding's campaign. If opponents could convince Americans that the charges were true, many would refuse to vote for him. Campaign officials condemned the reports as "base

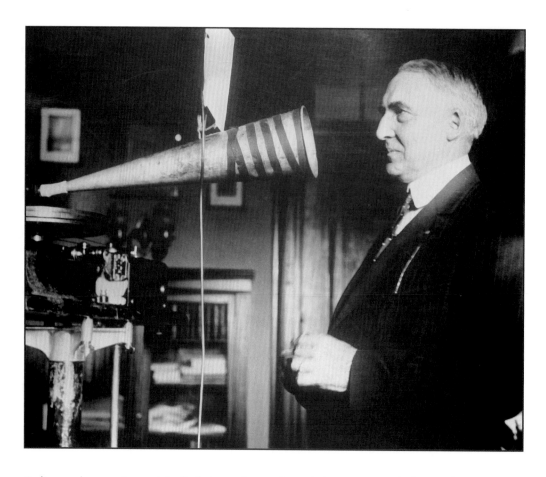

Harding records a campaign speech for distribution on phonograph records. His campaign was the first to make serious use of recorded speeches.

lies" and "mendacious slander." They published a *genealogy* showing that all of Harding's forebears were of European descent. Harding himself remained silent on the matter. He said that if he denied having black ancestors his statement would only add weight to the rumors.

Women cast their first votes in a presidential election.

Election day 1920 fell on November 2. It was also Warren Harding's 55th birthday. Florence Harding planned a surprise birthday party with a beautiful frosted cake. Harding's most cherished gift was a gold printer's rule from the employees of the *Star*. The rule was engraved with the date of the 1920 election,

Warren and Florence Harding wait to vote in Marion.

and space had been left for the date of Harding's re-election in 1924. By midnight the election results were in. Harding and Coolidge won a landslide victory. Harding received more than 16 million popular votes to Cox's 9 million. Warren G. Harding would become the 29th president of the United States.

Into the White House

From the start, Harding felt overwhelmed by his new responsibilities. In a letter to a friend he wrote, "I am just beginning to realize what a job I have taken over. God help me, for I need it."

Even before his inauguration Harding needed to choose his *cabinet*, the group of advisers who would help determine national policy in specific areas. Harding consulted with his political friends and supporters. He tried to find

Ohio, Mother of Presidents

Warren Harding was the last in a long line of U.S. presidents who were born in Ohio. Between 1868 and 1920, seven of the twelve men elected to the presidency had been Ohio natives. They included Ulysses S. Grant, Rutherford B. Hayes, James Garfield, Benjamin Harrison, William McKinley, and William Howard Taft. All of the Ohio presidents were Republicans. No other state except Virginia has sent so many men to the White House.

☆ ☆ ☆

persons of merit and loyal Republicans who would heal rifts in the party. He also hoped to appoint a few trusted friends, men who had supported him on his long political journey.

In December 1920, Harding announced Charles Evans Hughes of New York as his choice for secretary of state. Hughes was a lawyer who had served as governor of New York and as a justice in the U.S. Supreme Court. In 1916, he had been the Republican presidential candidate, losing the election to Woodrow Wilson. Hughes had a strong background in international relations and proved to be one of Harding's ablest cabinet members. Herbert Hoover accepted the position of secretary of commerce. One of the most admired men in America for his work to relieve hunger in Europe, Hoover would make the Commerce Department an important government agency. Banker Andrew W. Mellon became Harding's secretary of the treasury, where he helped reform the tax structure and reduce government spending.

Harding nominated his dedicated campaign manager, Will H. Hays, to serve as postmaster general. The postmaster general had the power to select people for jobs all across the country. Under Hays, most of these jobs went to faithful Republicans. Senator Albert Fall of New Mexico, another of Harding's close friends, became secretary of the interior. Finally, Harding appointed his longtime friend and champion, Harry Daugherty, as attorney general, the nation's highest

Harding with his vice president Calvin Coolidge (seated right), Secretary of Agriculture Henry Wallace and Secretary of Commerce Herbert Hoover. Coolidge and Hoover later served as president, and Wallace served as vice president.

law enforcement officer. As Harding's term in office progressed, some of these appointments proved disastrous.

On March 3, Harding said farewell to Marion. Schools, stores, and banks closed for an hour so that townspeople could see him off. Harding traveled in his special train car, the *Superb*, with his friends and family to Washington. The following day, March 4, 1921, he rode to the Capitol for the inauguration ceremony with outgoing president Woodrow Wilson in an automobile. It was the first time cars were used instead of horse-drawn carriages in the inaugural procession. On the East Portico of the Capitol Building, Harding repeated the solemn words of the presidential oath in his clear, ringing voice. Then he delivered his inaugural address. For the first time, a public address system carried his voice to the thousands of spectators.

During the last months of Wilson's term the White House had been cloaked in gloom. Because the president was ill, the mansion was closed to the public, and even private receptions were rare. Warren and Florence Harding ushered in a new era. They opened the grounds and lower floors to visitors, and delighted in meeting the public. Every day before lunch, no matter how busy he was, the president hosted an informal open house. Sometimes he shook hundreds of hands. Harding was enormously popular with the public and the press. Even his dog, a shaggy Airedale named Laddie Boy, became a celebrity.

Outgoing president Woodrow Wilson and incoming president Harding (both at left) ride to the inauguration ceremony on March 4, 1921.

Harding worked long hours during the day. He met with civic leaders, cabinet members, congressmen, and corporate officials. He drafted letters, speeches, and reports. Some of Harding's friends worried that he would push himself to exhaustion. He had had high blood pressure for years, but he refused to take it seriously. He once told a doctor that when his blood pressure was high, it was a sign that he wasn't working hard enough.

Harding also made time to relax. Twice a week he played golf, a game for which he developed a passion. Many evenings, he played poker with a group of friends, sometimes at the White House. Harding jokingly referred to this group of friends as his Poker Cabinet. Ned and Evalyn McLean, Albert Fall, Charles Forbes, Harry Daugherty, and Daugherty's assistant, Jess Smith, were among the regular players.

Harding's favorite pet Laddie Boy poses with a group of children on the White House lawn during the annual Easter Egg Roll.

Another close family friend and occasional poker player was Dr. Charles Sawyer, known to his friends as "Doc." The Hardings had brought Sawyer from Marion as the official White House physician. He had treated Florence Harding during her illness in 1905, and she had total faith in his abilities.

Harding brought his natural folksiness into the White House. He still chewed tobacco, though Florence strove to break him of the habit, and he smoked several cigars each day. He liked to sit with his feet propped on his desk while he talked to visitors in his office. He scandalized the dining-room staff by insisting that toothpicks be placed on the table at every meal.

The Chief Executive

Harding called a special session of Congress to meet in April 1921. In his address to the members, he outlined a series of programs that he hoped to advance during his administration. He asked for funding to maintain the nation's highways, and for government regulation of the radio industry. He urged the development of commercial air travel and suggested the establishment of a federal department to control air traffic. He recommended that Congress establish a Department of Welfare, which would cover education, health and sanitation, working conditions, and child welfare. He also suggested that the United States convert part of its large naval fleet to civilian use as a merchant marine. Finally, Harding declared that the United States must wipe out "the stain of barbaric lynching." Since the 1890s, more than 3,000 Americans had been *lynched*, or executed, by mobs without benefit of trial. At least 90 percent of the victims were African Americans.

The address was perhaps the most important speech Harding ever made. Even though he was conservative, he recommended innovative programs to help lead the nation into a changing modern world. Harding did not follow up his recommendations with pressure on Congress, however. Like many conservatives, he believed it was the role of Congress to make law and policy. Ordinarily, a

The Roaring Twenties

Harding promised a return to normalcy, but at the same time, the world was surging forward. Henry Ford and other automakers were offering cars at prices many families could afford, and for the first time, cars were choking the roads (most of which were not yet paved). Movie palaces were built in hundreds of towns and cities, attracting huge crowds, even though the movies themselves were still silent. Musical accompaniment was often provided by a theater pianist. Radio was becoming a source of information and entertainment to people in their homes.

New means of transportation and entertainment were adopted most eagerly by the young. The car made it easier for them to get together and "go out to the movies" at night and avoid parental supervision. The radio brought world news and the sounds of popular music to the smallest crossroads villages.

☆☆☆

Republican Congress would support the recommendations of a Republican president. The Congress of 1921 was dominated by Republicans, but the members did not work well together. Infighting between Republicans kept most of Harding's recommendations from being enacted.

With the help and advice of treasury secretary Mellon, Harding did gain passage of the Budget and Accounting Act in June 1921. It provided for the creation of the General Accounting Office and the Bureau of the Budget. The two agencies worked to ensure that government funds were handled properly, and to hold federal spending within limits. Mellon and Charles G. Dawes, the first director of the Budget Bureau, became experts at trimming wasteful spending. Dawes liked to say, "One cannot preach economy without practicing it." Together, they reorganized the government's planning and budgeting and reduced its expenses by billions of dollars.

Throughout his political career Harding supported big business. One of his favorite mottoes was, "Let's put less government in business, and more business in government." He favored policies that allowed businesses to operate with few restrictions. When major railroad and coal-mining strikes shook the nation in 1921, Harding took a strong anti-union stand. He argued that the strikers had a patriotic duty to settle their grievances, and he urged non-union strikebreakers to cross picket lines to help end the strikes. He seemed unwilling to consider the

Harding vacations with rubber tycoon Harvey Firestone. He also took vacation jaunts with car manufacturer Henry Ford and inventor Thomas Edison.

possibility that strikers' grievances were justified or that railroad and coal-mine owners might be partly responsible.

In one unexpected action, Harding released socialist and labor leader Eugene Debs from prison. Debs had been convicted of giving an anti-war speech in 1918 when the United States was at war in Europe and sentenced to ten years. In 1920, the Socialist party nominated him to run for president against Harding and Cox. Campaigning from prison, Debs won more than a million votes. Just before Christmas in 1921, Harding commuted Debs's sentence and ordered that he be freed.

Foreign Affairs

Harding entrusted issues of foreign policy to Secretary of State Charles Evans Hughes. Even though Republicans were on record against membership in the League of Nations, Hughes believed that the goal of international diplomacy was to avoid war, and he strove to enhance cooperation between the United States and other nations. Secretary of Commerce Herbert Hoover also had strong views on foreign policy. He believed that increasing world trade was an important way to assure peace in the world. He urged the United States to help war-torn and impoverished nations improve their economies to reduce the appeal of revolutionary ideas. He believed that revolutions like the one that made Russia a Communist nation in 1917 were caused by poverty and hunger.

Harding found it difficult to deal with so many complicated and controversial issues. When he received conflicting advice, he had trouble making a decision. Even though he worked hard as president, he often spent too much time on minor matters that were familiar to him and too little time on really important ones.

Harding places a wreath on the new casket of the unknown soldier who was buried two days later in the recently completed Tomb of the Unknown Soldier in Washington.

In one area, Harding was perfectly comfortable. He enjoyed the ceremonial role of the president. After World War I ended, Congress voted to memorialize an unknown U.S. soldier who had died in battle. On November 11, 1921, the third anniversary of the war's end, President Harding dedicated the Tomb of the Unknown Soldier at Arlington National Cemetery. With solemn dignity, he paid tribute to the Unknown Soldier and expressed his hope for lasting peace.

Chapter 6

By Friends Betrayed

By the spring of 1922, Harding was still popular with the American people. Congress and the cabinet viewed him with respect. "You and your administration give us strength and courage," Vice President Coolidge told him in a letter. Yet Harding himself was not quite content. Earlier, he had written in a personal letter, "Frankly, being President is rather an unattractive business unless one relishes the exercise of power. That is a thing which has never greatly appealed to me." He would soon learn that being president could be even more unattractive.

Harding had considered Charles Forbes to be one of his best friends ever since they met in Hawaii in 1915. In World War I, Forbes had achieved the rank of colonel. Harding appointed his friend to head the Veterans' Bureau in Washington. Thousands of wounded and disabled soldiers had returned to the United States at the end of World

War I, and there was a desperate need for new hospital space. The Veterans' Bureau was granted $500 million to build and operate the new veterans' hospitals. No other government bureau boasted so large a budget.

As head of the Veterans' Bureau, Forbes controlled that huge budget and government warehouses bursting with medical supplies. Forbes inspected the supplies and declared that they were damaged. He sold them at bargain prices to a Boston company, which secretly paid him a handsome reward for his generosity. Forbes then bought new supplies from other companies, paying ten times their actual value. This time, the sellers paid Forbes for allowing them to make such huge profits. He also mishandled the hospitals' supplies of alcohol, which was intended for medicinal use. He sold the alcohol to bootleggers, who used it to make illegal alcoholic beverages.

Soon Forbes announced plans for ten new veterans' hospitals. He gave the building contracts to friends in the construction business, allowing them to charge huge sums. They in turn gave gifts and payments to Forbes. As the money poured in, Forbes hosted lavish parties in Washington and Atlantic City. He rode in expensive cars, and dined in the finest restaurants.

Rumors of Forbes's corruption eventually reached President Harding. He called Forbes into his office and confronted him with the evidence. Usually

Harding was a gentle man who tried to avoid conflict. On this occasion he was so angry that he pushed Forbes against the wall and grabbed him by the neck, raging and shouting. Harding did not reveal the scandal, however. Hoping to avoid public disclosure, he accepted Forbes's resignation and sent him on a mission to Europe. Soon afterward a congressional investigation was begun, and it eventually calculated that Forbes cost the U.S. government more than $200 million. Harding was deeply hurt by Forbes's treachery. Florence Harding later wrote that her husband "never recovered from Forbes's betrayal of himself and the administration."

This was only the first rude shock to Harding. In May 1923, Jess Smith, Attorney General Daugherty's close friend and a member of Harding's Poker Cabinet, committed suicide. Before he died, Smith burned a bundle of papers in a metal wastebasket. Harding may have known what Smith had to hide. Daugherty was later tried for selling Justice Department favors for bribes. Whatever Harding knew, he took no action, and Daugherty remained in office.

In an unguarded moment with a journalist in 1923, Harding burst out, "I have no trouble with my enemies, I can take care of my enemies, all right. But my friends, my goddamn friends! They're the ones that keep me walking the floors nights."

The Voyage of Understanding ————————

Harding decided to leave the trouble of Washington behind to make a long, leisurely tour of the country. On June 20, 1923, a special ten-car train chugged out of Washington's Union Station. The *Superb*, carrying President Harding and the first lady, was the last car on the train. The presidential party included a congressman, a rear admiral, and a large supporting staff. Doc Sawyer was also aboard, along with his assistant, Dr. Joel T. Boone.

Harding called his two-month journey the Voyage of Understanding. He planned to travel to the West Coast, then north to Alaska. Along the way Harding planned to speak out about a new theme. He hoped to persuade voters that the United States should join the new Permanent Court of International Justice.

As part of the Treaty of Versailles, ending World War I, the signers established the League of Nations and a permanent court to consider legal disputes between nations. The U.S. Senate had refused to ratify the treaty, and the United States was not a member of the league or the permanent court. Harding hoped he could persuade the United States to join the court. He saw this as a way to make a mark on history, to lead the nation toward a better future.

The farther west he traveled, the more enthusiastic Harding's audiences became. Crowds lined the tracks as the train pulled into each station. People cheered and applauded. They waited in endless lines to shake his hand. Despite the summer heat, Harding always took the time to greet his supporters and well-wishers, but the trip was hard work. Even before he left Washington, Harding had been in poor health. Now he was near exhaustion. Yet Harding continued and never stopped shaking hands. At Tacoma, Washington, the presidential party boarded the USS *Henderson* for the four-day trip to Alaska. By now Secretary of Commerce Herbert Hoover had joined the expedition. One day Harding took Hoover aside.

"If you knew of great scandal in our administration," Harding asked, "would you for the good of the country and the party expose it publicly or would you bury it?"

Hoover replied, "Publish it, and at least get credit for integrity on your side."

Harding did not tell Hoover anything more, but clearly something was troubling him. Not even the beauty of Alaska's pristine coast, with its forests, glaciers, and unspoiled islands, seemed able to take his mind off his worries.

In 1923 Alaska had only 60,000 people, and Harding was the first president to visit the vast U.S. territory. He was dazzled by the landscape and charmed by the openness of the Alaskan people. Back aboard the *Henderson*, the presidential party headed south along the coast.

The Hardings during a cruise on their trip to Alaska in 1923.

★ THE LEGEND AND THE TRUTH ★

Tragedy

When Harding reached Seattle, he developed severe stomach cramps. He did not improve, and in San Francisco, Harding was moved into a suite at the Palace Hotel. For two days he seemed to be improving. Dr. Boone, however, remained concerned. He had discovered that the president had an enlarged heart and other signs of heart disease. Doc Sawyer did not agree. He insisted that food poisoning and exhaustion were the president's only problems.

On the evening of August 2, Florence Harding sat reading aloud by her husband's bedside. A few minutes after she left the room, Harding's nurse came in with a glass of water. She found him propped up on his pillows, looking relaxed and peaceful—but she saw in an instant that he was dead. The doctors who had attended Harding announced that he died of a stroke. Today most medical experts believe that the cause of death was a heart attack, and that Harding had untreated heart disease for a long time.

Nation in Mourning

The nation was stunned by the news. The whole country went into mourning. Harding's body was placed aboard the train that had carried him west on his Voyage of Understanding. Covered with black streamers, the train set off on its four-day journey back to Washington. In every city and town people lined the tracks to bid their president farewell.

In Washington, Harding's flag-draped coffin stood in the Capitol Rotunda. The new president, Calvin Coolidge, and a small group of family, friends, and top officials gathered around the coffin for a simple service. Then, for the next five hours, the Rotunda was open to the public. Thousands of people streamed past Harding's casket to pay their last respects.

That night Harding's body made its final journey by train from Washington to Marion, Ohio. As church bells tolled and weeping crowds looked on, pallbearers carried the coffin into the house on Center Street where Tryon Harding, the dead president's father, still lived. The next day Harding's pallbearers carried the casket to the Marion Cemetery. A girls' choir sang Harding's favorite hymn, "Lead, Kindly Light," and Harding's body was placed in a burial vault. At each side of the entrance stood a column crowned with an eagle. Three years before, those eagle-topped columns had stood along Harding's Victory Way.

Unraveling the Mysteries ——————————

After her husband's funeral in Marion, Florence Harding hurried back to the White House. As she cleaned out Harding's desk, she burned dozens of his letters

The funeral procession to honor Warren Harding in Marion, Ohio, where he was buried in 1923.

in his office fireplace. His remaining papers were shipped to Marion in ten enormous cartons, each one 10 feet (3 meters) long. There Florence Harding spent six weeks sorting through the contents. She burned any document she thought might damage her dead husband's reputation. When she was finished, the ten boxes of papers were reduced to only two.

Two months after Harding's death, the Senate launched an investigation into the oil leases of Teapot Dome. Teapot Dome was a strangely shaped sandstone formation near Casper, Wyoming. Beneath the dome lay a large supply of oil which the government had reserved for use by the U.S. Navy. (The navy was beginning to use oil instead of coal to fuel its ships.) In a national emergency, this reserve would insure it of a good supply. Demand for oil was also rising rapidly in the rest of the country. As automobiles grew more popular, oil would be needed to make gasoline. Oil companies looked forward to millions in profits.

Harding's secretary of the interior, Albert Fall, did not believe in government ownership of western lands. He believed that natural resources should be opened up to private industry. Fall got permission from Secretary of the Navy Edwin Denby to take over the management of military oil reserves. Then he secretly leased the right to drill for oil at Teapot Dome and other reserves to Harry Sinclair and Edward Doheny, friends who managed large oil companies. In return, Sinclair and Doheny gave Fall "gifts" amounting to more than $400,000.

Fall made a number of splendid improvements to his New Mexico ranch, and quietly resigned from Harding's cabinet in 1923.

In 1924, the investigation uncovered the whole ugly story. As one reporter put it, "The Senate investigation has become a 'gusher,' and both Republicans and Democrats . . . will carry the smell of petroleum." Secretary of the Navy Denby resigned. Albert Fall was eventually found guilty of bribery and served one year in prison. He was the first former cabinet member to serve a prison term for crimes committed while in office.

Another investigation involved the activities of former Veterans' Bureau chief Charles Forbes. Forbes protested his innocence to the end, insisting, "No man loved the ex-serviceman any better than I did." Nevertheless, the evidence piled up against him. In 1925 he was convicted of bribery and conspiracy and sentenced to spend two years in a federal penitentiary.

Investigations began to point at Harry Daugherty as well. Why had his friend Jess Smith committed suicide, and what were those papers he burned before his death? Smith had deposited $40,000 into Daugherty's account in an Ohio bank. The money was part of a bribe from the German owner of the American Metal Company. During the war, the U.S. government had taken over the company. Now the owner bribed Smith and others to help him establish a false claim and get it back. Daugherty destroyed records that involved the case

Former secretary of the interior Albert B. Fall (left) and oilman Edward Doheny (right) outside the courthouse after Fall was convicted of accepting bribes while serving in Harding's cabinet.

and was tried twice for obstructing justice, perhaps the most serious possible charge against an attorney general. Both trials resulted in hung juries, and Daugherty went free, but his reputation was tarnished forever.

There was no evidence that Harding ever accepted bribes or was involved directly in conspiracies. Yet some of his leading appointees had misused their power and betrayed the public trust to get rich. The Harding administration was tainted, and the taint spread to Harding himself. Surely, people said, he knew of the scandals seething around him, yet he never came forward. At the least he had shown poor judgment; at worst he covered up the truth to protect himself and his friends.

Harding's reputation was already tumbling in 1927, when Nan Britton published a memoir entitled *The President's Daughter*. The book described Britton's love affair with Harding and claimed that he was the father of her daughter Elizabeth Ann. It became an instant best seller. The public, it seemed, was hungry for tales that showed the former president in a bad light.

Remembering Warren Harding ——————

In the weeks after Harding's death, people across the country donated money to build the Harding Memorial in Marion. This enormous monument would house Harding's tomb. By 1927, when the memorial was completed, Harding's reputation had sunk so low that President Coolidge refused to participate in the dedication ceremony. As one journalist put it, Harding's memory had become "a rag in the gutter."

Looking back, most historians rank Harding as one of the least effective presidents in the nation's history. His record of accomplishments is very short. Worse, his failure to reveal the corrupt practices of his appointees places him in a class with President Ulysses S. Grant, whose administration 50 years earlier is considered the most corrupt in U.S. history.

The best that can be said is that Harding appointed a few honest and able men to high office. Secretary of the Treasury Mellon and Budget Director Dawes helped organize the country's finances and control its expenditures. Secretary of State Hughes made the first steps in repairing the international standing of the United States after its refusal to join the League of Nations. In addition, Harding himself proposed some positive programs. He spoke out in favor of federal support for highway construction, urged creation of a U.S. merchant marine, and spoke out courageously against the lynching of African Americans. Near the end of his life, he urged U.S. membership in the international court.

Sadly, he was rarely able to gain the support of Congress for his proposals, and accomplished very few of them. No action was taken against lynchings, and the United States did not join the World Court. Harding himself recognized

President Warren G. Harding.

his failings. A modest man at heart, he seemed to realize that the presidency revealed his weaknesses as a political leader and thinker.

To the end, Harding's strongest and most unshakable defender was Florence Harding. Even when she learned of his affairs with other women and of the corruption of his friends, she worked tirelessly to preserve his memory. Still suffering from the kidney ailments that had plagued her for years, Florence Harding died only 15 months after her husband, in November 1924.

In her last year, she helped preserve all that was positive of her husband's reputation. Imperfect as he was, she also missed him. She shared with her closest friends a poem she wrote after Warren Harding died. It includes the following lines:

In the graveyard softly sleeping,

Where the flowers gently wave,

Lies the one I loved so dearly,

And tried so hard to save. . . .

In my heart your memory lingers,

Tenderly fond and true,

There is not a day, dear husband,

That I do not think of you.

Fast Facts Warren G. Harding

Birth:	November 2, 1865
Birthplace:	Corsica, Ohio (now Blooming Grove)
Parents:	George Tryon Harding and Phoebe Dickerson Harding
Brothers & Sisters:	Charity Malvina (1867–?)
	Mary Clarissa (1868–1913)
	Eleanor Persilla (1872–1878)
	Charles Alexander (1874–1878)
	Abigail Victoria (1876–1935)
	George Tryon Jr. (1878–1934)
	Phoebe Caroline (1879–1951)
Education:	Ohio Central College, Iberia, Ohio; graduated 1882
Occupation:	Newspaper editor and publisher
Marriage:	To Florence Kling on July 8, 1891
Children:	None
Political Party:	Republican
Public Offices:	1900–1904 Member, Ohio State Senate
	1904–1906 Lieutenant Governor of Ohio
	1915–1921 Member, U.S. Senate
	1921–1923 29th President of the United States
His Vice President:	Calvin Coolidge (1921–1923)
Major Actions as President:	1921 Signed Budget and Accounting Act, establishing the Bureau of the Budget
	1921 Commuted prison sentence of socialist labor leader Eugene V. Debs
	1921 Dedicated the Tomb of the Unknown Soldier
	1923 Embarked on Voyage of Understanding to campaign for U.S. membership in World Court
Death:	August 2, 1923
Age at Death:	57
Burial Place:	Harding Memorial, Marion, Ohio

Fast Facts

Florence Kling Harding

Birth:	August 15, 1860
Birthplace:	Marion, Ohio
Parents:	Amos H. Kling and Louisa Bouton Kling
Brothers & Sisters:	None
Education:	Studied at the Cincinnati Conservatory of Music, Ohio
Marriages:	To Henry De Wolfe, March 1880 (divorced 1886)
	To Warren G. Harding, July 8, 1891
Children:	Marshall Eugene De Wolfe (1882–1915)
Death:	November 21, 1924
Age at Death:	64
Burial Place:	Harding Memorial, Marion, Ohio

Timeline

1865	1873	1882	1884	1884
Warren Gamaliel Harding is born in Corsica (present-day Blooming Grove), Ohio, November 2	The Harding family moves to Caledonia, Ohio	Harding graduates from Ohio Central College; settles with family in Marion, Ohio	With two friends, Harding acquires the Marion *Star*; soon becomes its sole editor	Attends the Republican National Convention in Chicago

1909	1912	1914	1916	1917
Harding defeated in campaign for governor of Ohio	Nominates William Howard Taft for president at Republican National Convention, June; Democrat Woodrow Wilson elected, November	World War I begins, August; Harding elected to the U.S. Senate from Ohio, November	Serves as chairman and keynote speaker at Republican National Convention; Woodrow Wilson re-elected	United States enters World War I

1923	1923	1924	1927	1930
Begins Voyage of Understanding to western states and Alaska, June	Harding dies in San Francisco, August 2; Calvin Coolidge sworn in as president	Congress begins investigation of Teapot Dome and other scandals in Harding administration; Florence Harding dies, November	A book by Nan Britton claims that Harding was the father of her child	Albert Fall convicted of receiving bribes in Teapot Dome scandal

1891	1899	1901	1903	1908
Marries Florence Kling, July 8	Elected to Ohio State Senate, re-elected in 1901	President William McKinley dies; Theodore Roosevelt becomes president	Elected Ohio lieu-tenant governor with Governor Myron Herrick	Ohioan William Howard Taft elected president

1918	1919	1920	1921	1921
Armistice ends World War I	Harding opposes United States membership in the League of Nations	Receives Republican nomination for president, June; elected president, November	Inaugurated president; March; addresses Congress, outlining legislative program, April	Signs Budget and Accounting Act, June; dedicates Tomb of the Unknown Soldier, November

1931

President Herbert Hoover dedicates the Harding Memorial in Marion, Ohio

Glossary

armistice: an agreement to end fighting in a battle or war while negotiations take place

bloviate: a slang term meaning to speak in a winning manner without saying anything significant

cabinet: in the U.S. government, the heads of federal departments who advise the president on national policy

conservative: in politics, believing that government should be restrained, leaving individuals and private organizations free to pursue their own goals

constituents: residents of a political district who are represented by an elected officeholder; these residents are the officeholder's constituents

delegate: a person who represents others at a convention or other meeting

genealogy: a document or diagram that shows a person's family tree

lynch: to execute a person accused of a crime without a trial

midwife: a person skilled in assisting women during childbirth

progressive: in politics, favoring action to reform or regulate business and government to protect or empower individuals

Prohibition: in U.S. history, the laws established under the 18th Amendment to the Constitution (1919), which prohibited the manufacture or sale of beverages containing alcohol; the amendment was repealed in 1933

stroke: blockage of blood flow in the brain, which can lead to paralysis and other disabilities

women's suffrage: in U.S. history, the movement to gain women the right to vote; the 19th Amendment to the Constitution (1920) granted women the right to vote in federal elections

Further Reading

Joseph, Paul. *Warren G. Harding: 29th President of the United States*. Edina, MN:
   Abdo Publishing, 1999.

Schultz, Randy. *Warren G. Harding*. Berkeley Heights, NJ: Enslow Publishers, 2003.

Somervill, Barbara A. *Warren G. Harding*. Minneapolis, MN: Compass Point, 2003.

Souter, Jerry. *Warren G. Harding: Our 29th President*. Chanhassen, MN: Child's World,
   2001.

MORE ADVANCED READING

Downs, Randolph C. *The Rise of Warren Gamaliel Harding, 1865–1920*. Columbus:
   Ohio State University Press, 1970.

Ferrell, Robert H. *The Strange Deaths of President Harding*. Columbia: University of
   Missouri Press, 1996.

Mee, Charles L. Jr. *The Ohio Gang: The World of Warren G. Harding*. New York: M.
   Evans & Co., 1981.

Russell, Francis. *The Shadow of Blooming Grove: Warren G. Harding in His Times*.
   New York: McGraw-Hill, 1968.

Sinclair, Andrew. *The Available Man: The Life Behind the Masks of Warren Gamaliel
   Harding*. New York: Macmillan, 1965.

Places to Visit

★ ★ ★ ★ ★

Warren Harding Home
380 Mount Vernon Avenue
Marion, OH 43302
(800) 600-6894
www.ohiohistory.org/places/harding

The fully restored home of Warren and
Florence Harding.

Harding Memorial
Marion, OH 43302
www.hardingfriends.org/pages/research/
memorial.htm

The memorial includes the tombs of
President Harding and his wife Florence
Kling Harding. For more information,
contact the Warren Harding Home (left).

The White House
1600 Pennsylvania Avenue NW
Washington, DC 20500
Visitors' Office: (202) 456-7041

The home of Warren and Florence Harding
from 1921 to 1923.

Online Sites of Interest

★ **Internet Public Library, Presidents of the United States (IPL POTUS)**

http://www.ipl.org/div/potus/wgharding.html

Includes concise information about Harding and his presidency; also provides links to other sites of interest.

★ **The American President**

http://www.americanpresident.org/history/warrenharding/

Provides valuable information on the life and times of U.S. presidents. Originally prepared from material for a public television series on the presidents, the site is now managed by the University of Virginia.

★ **The White House**

http://www.whitehouse.gov/history/presidents/wh29.html

Provides a brief biography of Warren Harding. The site also provides information on the current president, biographies of other presidents, and information on timely topics of interest.

★ **The American Presidency**

http://gi.grolier.com/presidents

Provides biographical information on the presidents at different reading levels, based on material in Scholastic/Grolier encyclopedias.

★ **Friends of Harding Home and Memorial**

http://www.hardingfriends.org/

Provides a brief biography of Harding.

★ **Harding in Marion**

www.shakerwssg.org/warren_g_hardingmarion_ohio.htm

Provides information on Marion, Ohio, and Harding's years there. Includes links to other sites of interest.

Table of Presidents

  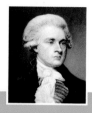 

	1. George Washington	2. John Adams	3. Thomas Jefferson	4. James Madison
Took office	Apr 30 1789	Mar 4 1797	Mar 4 1801	Mar 4 1809
Left office	Mar 3 1797	Mar 3 1801	Mar 3 1809	Mar 3 1817
Birthplace	Westmoreland Co, VA	Braintree, MA	Shadwell, VA	Port Conway, VA
Birth date	Feb 22 1732	Oct 20 1735	Apr 13 1743	Mar 16 1751
Death date	Dec 14 1799	July 4 1826	July 4 1826	June 28 1836

 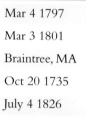

	9. William H. Harrison	10. John Tyler	11. James K. Polk	12. Zachary Taylor
Took office	Mar 4 1841	Apr 6 1841	Mar 4 1845	Mar 5 1849
Left office	Apr 4 1841•	Mar 3 1845	Mar 3 1849	July 9 1850•
Birthplace	Berkeley, VA	Greenway, VA	Mecklenburg Co, NC	Barboursville, VA
Birth date	Feb 9 1773	Mar 29 1790	Nov 2 1795	Nov 24 1784
Death date	Apr 4 1841	Jan 18 1862	June 15 1849	July 9 1850

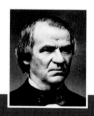  

	17. Andrew Johnson	18. Ulysses S. Grant	19. Rutherford B. Hayes	20. James A. Garfield
Took office	Apr 15 1865	Mar 4 1869	Mar 5 1877	Mar 4 1881
Left office	Mar 3 1869	Mar 3 1877	Mar 3 1881	Sept 19 1881•
Birthplace	Raleigh, NC	Point Pleasant, OH	Delaware, OH	Orange, OH
Birth date	Dec 29 1808	Apr 27 1822	Oct 4 1822	Nov 19 1831
Death date	July 31 1875	July 23 1885	Jan 17 1893	Sept 19 1881

5. James Monroe

6. John Quincy Adams

7. Andrew Jackson

8. Martin Van Buren

Mar 4 1817	Mar 4 1825	Mar 4 1829	Mar 4 1837
Mar 3 1825	Mar 3 1829	Mar 3 1837	Mar 3 1841
Westmoreland Co, VA	Braintree, MA	The Waxhaws, SC	Kinderhook, NY
Apr 28 1758	July 11 1767	Mar 15 1767	Dec 5 1782
July 4 1831	Feb 23 1848	June 8 1845	July 24 1862

13. Millard Fillmore

14. Franklin Pierce

15. James Buchanan

16. Abraham Lincoln

July 9 1850	Mar 4 1853	Mar 4 1857	Mar 4 1861
Mar 3 1853	Mar 3 1857	Mar 3 1861	**Apr 15 1865•**
Locke Township, NY	Hillsborough, NH	Cove Gap, PA	Hardin Co, KY
Jan 7 1800	Nov 23 1804	Apr 23 1791	Feb 12 1809
Mar 8 1874	Oct 8 1869	June 1 1868	Apr 15 1865

21. Chester A. Arthur

22. Grover Cleveland

23. Benjamin Harrison

24. Grover Cleveland

Sept 19 1881	Mar 4 1885	Mar 4 1889	Mar 4 1893
Mar 3 1885	Mar 3 1889	Mar 3 1893	Mar 3 1897
Fairfield, VT	Caldwell, NJ	North Bend, OH	Caldwell, NJ
Oct 5 1829	Mar 18 1837	Aug 20 1833	Mar 18 1837
Nov 18 1886	June 24 1908	Mar 13 1901	June 24 1908

	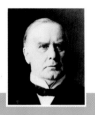			
	25. William McKinley	**26. Theodore Roosevelt**	**27. William H. Taft**	**28. Woodrow Wilson**
Took office	Mar 4 1897	Sept 14 1901	Mar 4 1909	Mar 4 1913
Left office	**Sept 14 1901•**	Mar 3 1909	Mar 3 1913	Mar 3 1921
Birthplace	Niles, OH	New York, NY	Cincinnati, OH	Staunton, VA
Birth date	Jan 29 1843	Oct 27 1858	Sept 15 1857	Dec 28 1856
Death date	Sept 14 1901	Jan 6 1919	Mar 8 1930	Feb 3 1924

	33. Harry S. Truman	**34. Dwight D. Eisenhower**	**35. John F. Kennedy**	**36. Lyndon B. Johnson**
Took office	Apr 12 1945	Jan 20 1953	Jan 20 1961	Nov 22 1963
Left office	Jan 20 1953	Jan 20 1961	**Nov 22 1963•**	Jan 20 1969
Birthplace	Lamar, MO	Denison, TX	Brookline, MA	Johnson City, TX
Birth date	May 8 1884	Oct 14 1890	May 29 1917	Aug 27 1908
Death date	Dec 26 1972	Mar 28 1969	Nov 22 1963	Jan 22 1973

	41. George Bush	**42. Bill Clinton**	**43. George W. Bush**	
Took office	Jan 20 1989	Jan 20 1993	Jan 20 2001	
Left office	Jan 20 1993	Jan 20 2001	—	
Birthplace	Milton, MA	Hope, AR	New Haven, CT	
Birth date	June 12 1924	Aug 19 1946	July 6 1946	
Death date	—	—	—	

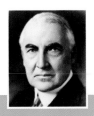

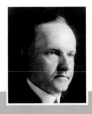

29. Warren G. Harding	30. Calvin Coolidge	31. Herbert Hoover	32. Franklin D. Roosevelt
Mar 4 1921	Aug 2 1923	Mar 4 1929	Mar 4 1933
Aug 2 1923•	Mar 3 1929	Mar 3 1933	Apr 12 1945•
Blooming Grove, OH	Plymouth, VT	West Branch, IA	Hyde Park, NY
Nov 21 1865	July 4 1872	Aug 10 1874	Jan 30 1882
Aug 2 1923	Jan 5 1933	Oct 20 1964	Apr 12 1945

37. Richard M. Nixon	38. Gerald R. Ford	39. Jimmy Carter	40. Ronald Reagan
Jan 20 1969	Aug 9 1974	Jan 20 1977	Jan 20 1981
Aug 9 1974★	Jan 20 1977	Jan 20 1981	Jan 20 1989
Yorba Linda, CA	Omaha, NE	Plains, GA	Tampico, IL
Jan 9 1913	July 14 1913	Oct 1 1924	Feb 6 1911
Apr 22 1994	——	——	June 5 2004

• Indicates the president died while in office.

★ Richard Nixon resigned before his term expired.

Index

Page numbers in *italics* indicate illustrations.

African Americans, 10, 25, 63–64, 74, 92
alcoholic beverages, 28, 45, 80
American Metal Company, 89
anti-Catholicism, 39
attorney general, 68, 70, 91
automobiles, 70, *71,* 74, 88

Blaine, James G., 17, 19
bloviating, 46
Boone, Joel T., 82, 85
bribery. *See* Corruption, political; Scandals
Britton, Nan, 47–49, *48,* 63, 91
Budget and Accounting Act (1921), 75
business, 27, 34, 54, 75

cabinet, presidential, 67–68, 89
Caledonia *Argus* (newspaper), 12
Chautauqua circuit, 34, 35, *36*
Christian, George, 49
Commerce, Department of, 68
communications technology, *64,* 70, 74
Congress, United States, 47, 74, 75, 92
conservatism, political, 27–28, 37, 54, 74
controversy, Harding's avoidance of
    party politics, 31, 33, 37
    presidency, 77
    public speaking, 46
    Senate, United States, 43, 45, 47
    Marion *Daily Star,* 28
Coolidge, Calvin, 57, *69,* 79, 86, 92
corruption, political, 63, 80–81, 88, 89, 91, 92
Court of International Justice, Permanent, 82,
    92
Cox, James M., 57, 63, 67

Daugherty, Harry M., *30, 32, 56, 72*
    attorney general, 68, 91
    corruption in administration, 81, 89, 91
    plans for Harding, 29–30, 54–55, 61
    presidency, opinion of, 54
Dawes, Charles G., 75, 92
De Wolfe, Henry, 23
death penalty, 28
Debs, Eugene, 76–77
Democratic Party, 57
Denby, Edwin, 88, 89
Doheny, Edward, 88
"Duchess" (nickname), 25

Easter Egg Roll at White House, *72*
election of 1920, popular vote, 57
Elizabeth Ann, 48, 63, 91

Fall, Albert, 68, 72, 88, 89, *90*
Firestone, Harvey, *76*
"folksy" style of Harding, 22, 61, 73
Foraker, Joe ("Fire Alarm Joe"), 31, *32,* 39
Forbes, Charles R., 41, 72, 79, 80, 81, 89
foreign policy, 77, 92
friends
    betrayal by, 81
    political life, part of, 16, 32, 33, 43, 68
    time spent with, 12, 15, 72
    Washington society, 49–50

Garfield, James, 61
General Accounting Office, 75
Grant, Ulysses S., 92

Hamilton, Alexander, 34
Hanna, Mark, 31, *32*

Harding, Florence Kling, *24, 44, 84*
  ambition, shared with Harding, 23, 37
  death, 94
  fast facts, 97
  illness, 34, 35, 73, 94
  marriages, 23, 25
  memory of president, 81, 94
  nicknamed "the Duchess," 25
  presidential papers, 86, 88
  wife of candidate, 59, 65, *66*
Harding, George Tryon (known as Tryon), *9,*
    14, 17, 19, 86
trades made by, 10, 12, 16
Harding, Phoebe, 8, *9,* 9–10
Harding, Warren G., *3, 5, 15, 66, 69, 76*
  campaign for president, *56,* 59–67, *60, 62,*
    64
  childhood and youth, 7–13, *11*
  conservatism of, 27–28, 74
  death and funeral, 85–86, *87*
  early jobs, 14–16, 17, 19
  fast facts, 96
  governor's race, 37–38
  health, 25–26, 55, 71, 73, 83, 85
  lieutenant governor, 33–34
  marriage, 25
  newspaperman, 12, 13, 16, 17, 19–21, 22
  nomination for president, 54–57
  presidency, 67–85, 71, *84, 93*
  reputation, 79, 88, 91, 92
  senator from Ohio, 39, 41, 43, *44,* 45, 47
  state senator, 29, 31–33, *33*
  timeline, 98–99
Harding Memorial, 91–92
Harmon, Judson, 38
Hays, Will H., 61, 63, 68
Herrick, Myron, 33, 34
Hogan, Timothy S., 39, 41

Hoover, Herbert, 68, *69,* 77, 83
hospitals, veterans', 80
Hughes, Charles Evans, 68, 77, 92

Iberia *Spectator* (newspaper), 13

Kling, Amos, 23, 25
Kling, Florence. *See* Harding, Florence Kling

labor, 27–28, 75–76
Laddie Boy, 70, *72*
League of Nations, 51, 52, *62,* 82
legislative proposals of Harding, 45, 73, 92
Lodge, Henry Cabot, 51
Longworth, Alice Roosevelt, 49, *50*
Longworth, Nicholas, 49, *50*
love letters written by Harding, 35, 47, 48
Lowden, Frank, 54, 55
lynchings, 74, 92

Marion, Ohio, 7, 8, 14, 26
  burial of Harding, 86, *87,* 91–92
  house built by Hardings, *26*
  popularity of Harding, 31, 38, 59–61, 70
  promotion by Harding, 21–23
  Star building, *20*
Marion *Daily Star*, 16, 17, 22, 26, 65
  building, *20*
  Florence Harding, business manager, 25
  improvements made by Harding, 19–21
Marion *Mirror*, 19
Marion *Weekly Star*, 21
McAdoo, William, 46
McKinley, William, 31, 45, 61
McLean, Evalyn, 49–50, 72, 73
McLean, Ned, 72
Mellon, Andrew W., 68, 75, 92
merchant marine, 73, 92

motion pictures, 74
mule ride to Marion, 7–8, 13

Navy, United States, 73, 88
nervous breakdowns, 25–26

Ohio, 31–33, 61, 67
Ohio Central College, 12–13
oil reserves, government, 88

Phillips, Carrie, 35, 37, 47, 63
Phillips, Jim, 35, 37, 63
Poker Cabinet, 72
poker games, 15, 19, 33
postmaster general, 68
President's Daughter (book, Britton), 49, 91
presidents from Ohio, 67
printer's rule, 12, 65
Progressive Party, 39
progressives, political, 37, 57. *See also*
       Reform movements
Prohibition, 28, 45, 80
public speaking, 13, 29, 39, 46

radio, 73, 74
railroads, 17, 61, 63, 70, 75, 82
reform movements, 28, 45, 57. *See also*
       Progressives, political
Republican party
    1884 National Convention, 17, *18*
    1912 National Convention, 38–39, *40*
    1916 National Convention, 45–46
    1920 nomination process, 54–57
    divisions in national party, 37, 54, 75
    Ohio, 31, 33, 67
"Roaring Twenties," 74
Roosevelt, Alice (later Longworth), 49, 50
Roosevelt, Theodore, 37, 39, 52, 61

Sawyer, Charles, 73, 82, 85
scandals
    administration, 81, 83, 88–89, 91
    personal, 47, 63, 91
Senator (dog), 22
Sickle, Johnnie, 19
Sinclair, Harry, 88, *90*
Smith, Jess, 72, 81, 89
Spectator (newspaper), 13

Taft, William Howard, 37, 38, 39
Teapot Dome, 88–89
Tomb of the Unknown Soldier, 78
trade, international, 77
transportation, 73, 92. *See also* Automobiles;
    Railroads

Unknown Soldier, 78, *78*

Versailles, Treaty of, 82
Veterans' Bureau, 79, 80
Voyage of Understanding, 82, *84*

Wadsworth, James, Jr., 43
Wallace, Henry, *69*
Warwick, Jack, 19, 28
Washington, D.C., 41, 49
Welfare, Department of, 73
White House, 70, *72,* 73
Wilson, Woodrow, 39, *53,* 61, 70, *71*
    League of Nations, 51
    stroke, 52
    World War I, 47, 63
Winnie (nickname), 8
women's suffrage, 25, 45, *65*
Wood, Leonard, 52, 54, 55
World Court, 82, 92
World War I, 46, 47, 51, 78, 82

About the Author

Deborah Kent grew up in Little Falls, New Jersey. She received her B.A. in English from Oberlin College in northeastern Ohio, not far from Harding's boyhood home. She earned a master's degree from Smith College School for Social Work.

After four years as a social worker at the University Settlement House in New York City, Ms. Kent moved to San Miguel de Allende in Mexico to try her hand at writing. While living in Mexico she completed her first novel, *Belonging*. Ms. Kent is the author of 18 young-adult novels and numerous non-fiction titles for middle-grade readers. She lives in Chicago with her husband, children's-book author R. Conrad Stein, and their daughter Janna.

Photographs © 2004: Art Resource, NY/National Portrait Gallery, Smithsonian Institution, Washington, DC: cover back, 5, 93, 99 bottom; Brown Brothers: 9 left, 9 right, 11, 20, 32 right, 32 left, 36, 40, 65, 69, 98 top left, 98 top right; Corbis Images: 15, 24, 48, 50, 53, 64, 98 bottom center, 99 center left, 99 top left (Bettmann), 26, 102 (Layne Kennedy), 18, 78, 87, 98 bottom left, 99 center far right; Hulton|Archive/Getty Images: 33, 44, 90, 98 bottom right, 99 top right; Library of Congress: cover, 3 (via SODA), 71, 72, 99 center right; Ohio Historical Society: 30, 56, 60, 62, 66, 76, 99 center far left; UCR/California Museum of Photography, University of California, Riverside/Ketstone-Mast Collection: 84.

Table of Presidents photographs copyright © 2004 Library of Congress, except for George W. Bush copyright © 2004 www.RightNews.com

4/0 9 ②
5/14 ③